A Book of Your Own

A Book of Your Own

Keeping a Diary or Journal

Carla Stevens

CLARION BOOKS
New York

Clarion Books
a Houghton Mifflin Company imprint
215 Park Avenue South, New York, NY 10003
Text copyright © 1993 by Carla Stevens

Library of Congress Cataloging-in-Publication Data
Stevens, Carla.
A book of your own : keeping a diary or journal / Carla Stevens.
p.   cm.
Summary: Discusses diaries and journals and how to keep one,
providing instructions, examples, and excerpts from journals both
famous and obscure.
ISBN 0-89919-256-4   PA ISBN 0-395-67887-0
1. Diaries—Authorship—Juvenile literature.   [1. Diaries.]
I. Title.
PN4390.S74   1993
808'.06692—dc20
92-33818
CIP   AC
BP   10   9   8   7   6   5   4   3   2   1

For the next generation of diarists—
Adam and Robin; Raphael and Lily

Acknowledgments

Excerpts from the following books have been used with permission: *The Diary of Helena Morley*, Elizabeth Bishop, editor, copyright © 1957 by Elizabeth Bishop, published in 1977 by The Ecco Press. *Anne Frank: The Diary of a Young Girl* by Anne Frank, copyright © 1967 by Doubleday, a division of Bantam, Doubleday, Dell Publishing Group, Inc. *Growing Pains* by Wanda Gág, copyright © 1940 by Wanda Gág, copyright renewed © 1967 by Robert Janssen. Reprinted by permission of Coward McCann, Inc. *The Journal of Beatrix Potter* by Leslie Linder, copyright © Frederick Warne, London, 1966. *With Sherman to the Sea: The Civil War Letters, Diaries and Reminiscences of Theodore F. Upson*, copyright © Oscar Osburn Winther, Louisiana State University Press, 1943.

The author acknowledges her debt to the authors of two biographies of E. B. White for information about his life: Scott Elledge, *E. B. White: A Biography*, published by W. W. Norton Company, New York, in 1984 and Beverly Gherman, author of *E. B. White, Some Writer!*, published by Atheneum, New York, in 1992.

A Note of Thanks

This book could not have been written without the generosity of my family and friends who gave me permission to share some of their diary entries with you. I especially want to thank Elizabeth Ames, Christianne Deschamps, Charlayne Evans, Tanya Golembeski, Michael Karp, Abby Kessler, Doris Klein, Sebastian Lousada, Matthew O'Grady, Christopher Pratt, April Stevens, Sara Stevens, and Steven Warren.

Many of the ideas presented here have been tried out in my journal writing classes at the New School in New York City. I owe a great deal to my students whose honesty and courage so movingly revealed in their diaries has enriched my life.

Finally, I want to thank James Giblin, my editor and friend, for his invaluable comments throughout the stages of this book.

—C.S.

Contents

Introduction

Amsterdam, Holland
June 12, 1942

I hope I shall be able to confide in you completely as I have never been able to do in
anyone before, and I hope you will be a great
support and comfort to me.

ANNE FRANK, age 13
(from *Anne Frank: The Diary of a Young Girl*)

This book is about diaries and journals and about how to
keep a diary or journal of your own. Writing in a diary is
not like writing to a friend or completing an assignment
for school. You don't have to worry about spelling or what
your handwriting looks like, nor do you have to worry
about what others will think of you. You write only to
please yourself.

Each of us is eager to discover as much as we can of the

truth about ourselves, and this quest for self-understanding continues all our lives. Writing can be an important part of the process of growing. Your diary can make you aware of the inner riches you already possess. It can be a creative force for you, recharging your spirit and encouraging you to be more daring and imaginative.

For a long time people have used diaries and journals to record their most private thoughts and to describe experiences that were important to them. The diary and journal excerpts you will read in the following pages were written by young people who lived in different parts of the world and at different times.

But whether the young diarists lived one hundred years ago or in the present, in England or in Massachusetts, you will soon discover they are much like yourself. Scattered among the day-to-day events that caught their attention at the moment are their pleasures and disappointments, dreams and self-doubts—feelings that link us all, one to another.

Some of the excerpts you will read come from published books like *Anne Frank: The Diary of a Young Girl.* Others are from private diaries kept by family members and friends who were willing to share them with you. Many were discovered and published after their authors grew up or died. The original spelling and punctuation have been retained, even when incorrect.

If you do not lose or destroy your diary, someday you may value much of what you wrote when you were young and wish to share it with others. Perhaps you will even tuck your diary away in a safe place for the next generation to discover and enjoy!

Rochester, New York
January 6, 1864

Think I froze the big toe on my left foot today when I went out. Maybe I can work it to stay out of school. Changed the pocketbook Ma give me for Chrismas for a bigger one. Hope I shall need it. If I freeze all my toes one at a time maybe I can stay out of school for pretty near two weeks. Hope it don't get warm.

JAMES H. THOMPSON, age 10
(from *The Real Diary of a Rochester Boy*)

James Thompson's original notebook was found in a heap of old books in a secondhand dealer's shop. Throughout his tenth year, the young author faithfully recorded the events of his life. The Civil War, which was raging at the time, was of little interest to him. He was much more concerned with his battles at school and at home.

~ 1 ~

A Book of Your Own

Salem, Massachusetts
May 7, 1854

I feel that keeping a diary will be a pleasant and profitable employment of my leisure hours and will afford me much pleasure in after years, by recalling to my mind the memories of other days, thoughts of much-loved friends from whom I may then be separated, with whom I now pass many happy hours; the interesting books that I read; and the different people, places, and things that I am permitted to see. Besides this, it will doubtless enable me to judge correctly of the growth and improvement of my mind from year to year.

CHARLOTTE FORTEN, age 16
(from *The Journal of Charlotte Forten*)

Charlotte Forten was a member of a distinguished black family in Philadelphia. Her father, a sailmaker, sent her to Salem, Massachusetts, so that she could be educated in unsegregated schools. During the Civil War, on the Sea Islands off the coast of South Carolina, she taught many freed slaves to read.

In this book, *diary* and *journal* refer to a series of dated writings jotted down in private moments. *Diary* comes from the word *diarium,* meaning "daily allowance" in Latin, and *journal* comes from the French word *journal,* meaning "daily."

Whatever you choose to call your book, you need not think you must write in it every single day. Perhaps you will write every day for a while, then for some reason you will write less often. But if you keep coming back to your writing, you will have the satisfaction of seeing yourself change and grow over time. This is one of the rewards of keeping a personal journal.

Bridgewater, Connecticut
November 27, 1973

It's Nov. 27 almost 27 days since I last wrote. I'll try to write every day. I want to write about life and about my home. I love this house and all the animals. This house will never stop with the music and the doors opening and shutting. It won't stop till the end of the world. Today I saw a newborn calf only an hour old. I wondered how he felt to just come into the world. Elizabeth went home Sunday. I got home after she left and spilt my lunch on the floor. Mom yelled at me. I cryed for 15 minutes. I guess that was the first time I had ever been lonesome. It's a bad feeling.

APRIL STEVENS, age 10

April grew up in a small rural village in New England. She began to keep a diary when she was seven years old, a practice she still continues today.

A diary entry is like a snapshot. It may be out of focus at times, but it still catches your spirit and character better than any formal portrait. When you are seventeen or twenty or forty-five, what will you think when you look back at the entries you wrote when you were nine or ten? Rereading your diary can help you to find your way back to your younger self. But of course this assumes that you have not abandoned your journal for too long.

Queens, New York
August 1, 1914

I am 11 years old. I know I am not serious enough. Last night I said to myself: tomorrow I will be good. Good? I wasn't any better than I was the day before. Now here is a new month, and I haven't yet thought out how to master my impulses and my temper . . . Today is nearly over and it isn't much, but for the rest of the day I will observe silence. Not talk but answer politely. Not seek out conversation but

work on my shawl which must be finished by
at least the day after tomorrow.

ANAÏS NIN, age 11
(from *Linotte: The Early Diary of Anaïs Nin*)

Anaïs Nin was born in Paris in 1903. When she was eleven, after her father abandoned the family, her mother took her and her two brothers to America to seek a better life. Anaïs began keeping a diary for her father "so he could follow us into a strange land and know about us." But before long she switched to writing English, a language her father could not read. In 1966, when Anaïs was sixty-three years old, the first of six diaries was published and she immediately became famous.

Devon, England
January 15, 1905

I am thinking that on the whole I am a most discontented mortal. I get fits of what I call "what's the use of anything" mania. I keep asking myself incessantly till the question wears me out. What's the good of going into the country naturalizing? What's the good of studying so hard? Where is it going to end? Will it lead anywhere?

W. N. P. BARBELLION, age 15
(from *The Journal of a Disappointed Man*)

W. N. P. (Wilhem Nero Pilate) Barbellion's real name was Bruce Frederick Cummings. From early childhood he was interested in natural science. He began to keep a journal when he was twelve. When he grew up, he became a respected biologist. He is most famous for his diary, however, which was published with a note of the author's death on December 31, 1917. But Barbellion had prepared the diary for publication himself! He lived two more years and died in 1919 when he was twenty-nine years old.

A Book to Write In

You can write in a book made specifically for diarists that contains a blank page for each day of the year. Often these books have a lock and key. If you don't wish to write every single day, though, you may prefer a book with blank pages that you can date yourself. Anne Frank wrote in a small, red-checkered clothbound notebook that had lined pages.

Noah Blake kept a diary from March 25, 1805, to the following Christmas. In those days, there were no books with blank pages for sale. You had to make your own. The pages of Noah's diary were made at a local paper mill. He bound them in calfskin and wrapped them once around with a leather thong. He made his own ink by mashing and boiling walnut hulls and adding a little vinegar and salt. Then he dipped a crow quill feather into the ink and began to write:

> Noah Blake, my book
> March the twenty-fifth year of Our Lord, 1805
> Given to me by my Father Izaak Blake and my

Mother Rachel upon the fifteenth year of my
Life.

We can still read what Noah wrote almost two hundred
years ago. If you hope to have your diary for a long time,
be sure to write with a pen because most pencil marks
smudge and fade.

Today you can choose your diary from among bound
books of all shapes and sizes. Even a loose-leaf notebook
can become a useful diary, for it is easy to tear out a page
when you want to discard an entry or share something
with a friend. You can type your entries and keep them in
a folder labeled *Journal*. You may even prefer to write on
your computer. But the advantage of a notebook is that
you can tuck it in your pocket or knapsack and take it with
you anywhere.

Keeping Your Diary Private

If you are honest, your journal will contain glimpses of
you that you won't want to reveal to others. At one time
you may be very angry at a family member you are sup-
posed to love. At another time you may have a secret that
you don't want anyone to know about. When you write in
your journal, your purpose is not to hurt or upset others.
Your purpose is to record openly, without fear of exposure, your deepest, innermost thoughts and feelings so
that you can understand yourself better.

How can you be sure that others won't read what you
write in your diary? You really cannot be one hundred
percent sure. Perhaps you should first discuss keeping a

journal with your parents. Ask them to respect your privacy by not reading it. But even then, don't leave your journal around to tempt others. Put it out of sight, in a good hiding place—for example, behind books on your bookshelf or tucked away in a dark corner of your closet. You may even wish to keep your diary in a box with a lock and key.

If you decide that you cannot trust those around you to respect your privacy, then write your most private thoughts on a separate sheet of paper that you can tear up later if you wish. It can be very upsetting to discover that someone has read your diary uninvited.

> *Cairo, Illinois*
> *Friday, June 24, 1881*
> But oh, I'm white-hot with indignation. All of us went to the funeral and while we were gone, Sallie and Jennie Hinkle came over and read you through and through. . . . Oh, the enormity of the meanness! The more I look back and read what they read, the madder I get. To think! When I wouldn't even let my own mother, Elmore, Edith, not my dearest friend read it! And then these girls without even a "May I please?" reading it all. I'll never like them again. My Journal is ME the innermost part of me and to think of—MAUD SHUT UP OR YOU'LL FLY INTO INCH PIECES. All right.
>
> ISABELLA MAUD RITTENHOUSE, age 14
> (from *Maud*)

Isabella Maud Rittenhouse was born in Cairo, Illinois, in 1867. She started a journal when she was twelve years old and kept it regularly until she was thirty. Later she burned the first volume, but six others followed, each containing more than 100,000 words. In 1939, when she was seventy-two, she agreed to have a selection of her diaries published. "Maud" always wrote in purple ink and poured her heart out to her "dear Grandame Journal."

Getting Started

Are you ready to begin? If you are, then write the day, the date, and the year on top of the page. Be sure to do this each time you sit down to write. A year from now, it will be all too easy to forget what you were doing at this time if you don't record the date. Now begin with what is happening at the moment.

Rochester, New York
January 1, 1864

It's 5 degrees below zero and we had oyesters and company today. The oyesters was good. Played a game of uker [cards; correct spelling, *euchre*] on the sly. I am going to keep this diary this year or bust. Last year I stopped in March. I have got it locked in a box in my room. A diary aint much good unless you keep it.

JAMES H. THOMPSON, age 10
(from *The Real Diary of a Rochester Boy*)

Your diary entry can vary in length from one word to one page to ten pages or more. Write big, write little—neatly, messily—any which way on the page. It doesn't matter how you spell or whether your grammar is correct or how you organize and arrange your thoughts. Your only audience is yourself.

Clark, New Jersey
January 1, 1977

I, Abby Kessler do solemnly swear to keep this diary every day during the year of 1977 in order to save my mental sanity. Please forgive and understand when I use obscene language as I can't keep from spilling out as my mother well knows. Be my friend, diary. I need one!

ABBY KESSLER, age 13

When my friend Abby sent me excerpts from her diary, she wrote: "My thirteenth year was the most difficult of my life. My grandfather had just died and I was uprooted and moved to a strange town and a new junior high school in the middle of the fall term."

There is no limit to what you can put in your journal. You can tape in ticket stubs and four-leaf clovers, write poems and stories, make lists, and draw pictures. You can write about anything—from the weather to gossip to a fight with your parents—everything that affects or moves you in some way. The more you include of the bits and pieces of your life, the more interesting and useful your diary will be to you.

Benjamin Musser began to keep a diary in 1901 when he was twelve years old and he continued until he got married in 1921. By that time he had filled nearly eighty volumes, padded with theater tickets and programs, letters, and drafts of his stories and poems. In addition, he made innumerable drawings in the margins.

This is the way he began:

THE JOURNAL OR DIARY
OF
BENJAMIN MUSSER, JOURNIOR

I hereby dedicate this journal, (however illiterate it may be, for I hope the recipient will forgive all that) to my Conscience and my brother Fred.

Philadelphia, Pa.
October 11, 1901

This morning while cleaning out my closet I came across this book. I have perfect rafts of blank books, scrapbooks and the like, all well filled, so I wondered what I should do with this . . . Then I thought of having a journal or diary, and we shall now commence. Doubt if I shall ever let anyone see this, except chums and perhaps Fred and Julia [his sister], for the writing is fierce.

BENJAMIN MUSSER, age 12
(from *The Diary of a Twelve Year Old*)

New York City
August 6, 1849

I am ten years old today, and I am going to begin and keep a diary. My sister says it is a good plan, and when I am in a remembering mood, I can take my diary and read about what I did when I was a little girl.

CATHERINE ELIZABETH HAVENS
(from *The Diary of a Little Girl in Old New York*)

Catherine Havens was eighty years old and in a remembering mood in 1920 when she showed her diary to a publisher. He was delighted by it and turned it into a book.

A Diary Called Kitty

The idea of addressing your diary as if it were an imaginary friend is not unusual. After all, it is almost like a friend to whom you can confide your secret thoughts. Perhaps, like Anne Frank and Doris Klein, you will want to give your diary a name.

Amsterdam, Holland
June 20, 1942

And now I come to the root of the matter, the reason for starting a diary: it is that I have no such real friend . . . In order to enhance in my mind's eye the picture of the friend for whom I have waited for so long, I don't want to set down a series of bald facts in a diary like most people do, but I want this diary itself to be my friend and I shall call my friend Kitty.

ANNE FRANK, age 13
(from *Anne Frank: The Diary of a Young Girl*)

Anne Frank's diary, which she kept while hiding from the Nazis in an attic in Amsterdam, is perhaps the most famous diary published in this century. Anne died in a concentration camp when she was fifteen years old.

January 24, 1931

Diary, you are a truly beautiful book, and you are colored in one of my favorite colors, blue. True Blue—that's what I would like to call you. Now that you are properly named, suppose we begin our secrets—but one minute, before we do this—we both must swear never to let anyone know what is in these pages—is it a go? All right.

DORIS KLEIN, age 14

Doris Klein says that her favorite place for writing in her diary was the bathroom because no one bothered her there. She still has all the diaries she kept when she was an adolescent. Today she is an artist who lives in New York City.

Once you begin, you will discover that there is suspense in keeping a diary. At most you know what to write about today, but you cannot know what you will write about tomorrow or the day after that. Each entry will be different because your life changes from moment to moment, year after year. And you change too. Your journal will reflect you in all your complexity.

Exeter, New Hampshire
December 7, 1868

Got sent to bed last nite for smoking hayseed cigars and can't go with Beany any more. It is funny, my father won't let me go with Beany because he is tuf, and Pewt's father won't let Pewt go with me because I'm tuf, and Beany's father says if he catches me or Pewt in his yard he will lick time out of us. Rainy today.

HENRY AUGUSTUS SHUTE, age 12
(from *The Real Diary of a Real Boy*)

Henry was born in Exeter, New Hampshire, in 1856. When he grew up he became a judge in his hometown. One day while he was cleaning out an old closet he found the diary he kept when he was a boy. The diary was first published as a serial in his local newspaper. It attracted the attention of a publisher in Boston who turned the serial into a book called The Real Diary of a Real Boy, *and it became a bestseller.*

~ 2 ~

Lists, Wishes, and Secret Thoughts

Walden Pond
Massachusetts, 1844

I should not talk so much about myself if there was anybody else I knew as well.

HENRY DAVID THOREAU, age 27
(from *Walden*)

For two years Henry David Thoreau lived alone in a cabin he built himself. He fished and swam, read a lot, and talked to his friends. His simple, independent way of life gave him time to think about all kinds of things, and he recorded in his "day book" not only what he observed in nature but how he felt and what he believed. Fifty years after his death in 1862, his journal was published. Today it is read and admired by people all over the world.

Keeping a diary helps you to observe more and respond more to what is taking place around you. Sometimes after going through what you think is your most boring day, you will sit down and write on and on and on. Instead of recording all the things that happened on that day, you begin to reflect on your life. Thoughts seem to come to you effortlessly. Writing during these times is almost like daydreaming.

At other times, writing about a situation that puzzles or troubles you can help to clarify your thinking and make it easier to know what to do. It is satisfying when you can work something out for yourself.

Friday the thirteenth (Nov., 1901)

And it was sort of unlucky too. I had a scrap with one of the fellows at the game, a real fist fight, and he beat me all right. I don't seem to be a born fighter and haven't much strength. I don't even know what the fight was about, except he said I was a sissy and couldn't fight, and I said I could, and then he jumped on me and pounded me just because he was bigger and knew he could lick me . . . But what did he gain by fighting me when he knew he was bigger and stronger before he started it? I don't believe in wars anyway and I never will as long as I live, so help me God. They don't prove anything and are just savages under our selves fighting like wild animals and they don't know why or anything.

BENJAMIN MUSSER, age 12
(from *The Diary of a Twelve Year Old*)

Bridgewater, Connecticut
November 23, 1974

I bet you've never been laughed at or lonesome or ever been left out. No I didn't think
so. How would you like eating your lunch all
alone? All alone at one seperate table while
friends sit all around you. Sat around with
there various boy friends. I've never had one.
Never, ever, and I guess I never will. I mean
what's the use of life when most of the time
you would rather die than live with all this cru-
elty.

"Oh but your a great kid—everybody likes
you." Yeah, but who—just tell me who?

APRIL STEVENS, age 10

Wishing

Once a year, you make a secret wish before blowing out
the candles on your birthday cake. But you can make
wishes far more often in your diary. You can make a wish
once a week, or even once a day if you want to! After a
while, it will be fun to check back and see which of your
wishes came true.

When you are feeling playful and inventive, your
wishes can be funny, fantastic, and impossible.

I wish I was the smartest person in the world.
I wish I could talk cat language.
I wish I could turn into a horse and then back again.
I wish all my wishes would come true!

When you are feeling more thoughtful, your wishes will reflect your secret dreams.

> I wish I had a best friend.
> I wish I could stop biting my nails.
> I wish Mom and Dad would stop fighting.
> I wish I could get a part in *Bye, Bye Birdie.*

Resolutions

Sometimes there is not too much you can do to make a wish come true. A list of your intentions, on the other hand, can help you to get things accomplished and remind you of the kind of person you hope to be. When Benjamin Franklin was twenty years old, in 1726, he kept a journal in which he made a plan for "regulating my future in life." Years later, Franklin stressed the value of having made those resolutions when he was young, for they helped to shape his character.

1. It is necessary for me to be extremely frugal for some time til I have paid what I owe.

2. [I must] endeavor to speak the truth in every instance and aim at sincerity in every word and action—the most amiable excellence in a rational human being.

3. [I must] apply myself industriously to whatever business I take in hand, and not divert my mind from my business by any foolish project of growing suddenly rich; for industry and patience are the surest means of plenty.

4. I resolve to speak ill of no man whatever, · not even in a matter of truth; but rather by some means excuse the faults I hear charged upon others and upon proper occasions speak all the good I know of everybody.

The beginning of the New Year is usually a time to think back about the year that has passed and to think ahead about the year to come. Many people make a list of the changes they hope to make in the new year. You too can list your New Year's resolutions in your diary. A year later, when you look back, you can see how many resolutions you kept.

New Ulm, Minnesota
January 1, 1908

1. Resolved that I shall try to make the next year brighter and pleasanter.

2. That I shall try to do neater and better work at school.

3. Resolved that I shall try to keep my things properly mended.

4. Resolved that I shall try to have more patience with my sisters and especially my brother.

5. Resolved that I shall try not to worry any more than is necessary and to skip over troubles as lightly as possible.

6. Resolved that I shall try to practise more on the piano and not such easy 1, 2, 3, 4 ones either. Good ones, I mean.

7. Resolved that I must try and not forget to clean my teeth every day.

WANDA GÁG, age 15
(from *Growing Pains*)

Wanda Gág began to keep a diary when she was fifteen years old and she continued it for over thirty years. When she grew up, she became an artist and an author/illustrator of books for children. Millions of Cats *is still read and loved by children all over the world.*

London, England
January 7, 1798

I have known my faults and not corrected them and now I am determined I will once more try to overcome my wicked inclinations.

I must not flirt.

I must never be out of temper with the children.

I must not mump when my sisters are liked and I am not.

I must not allow myself to be angry.

I must not be idle in my mind.

I must try to give way to every good feeling and overcome every bad.

ELIZABETH GURNEY FRY, age 17
(from *Elizabeth Fry, Quaker Heroine*)

Betsy Gurney was born in 1780, one of twelve children in a Quaker family. When she was nineteen, she married Joseph Fry, a Quaker banker, and they eventually had eleven children. She devoted most of her life to reforming the terrible prison conditions for women which existed in England at that time.

Lists

Everyone makes lists—shopping lists, lists of things to do and people to call. A list can be a time-saver and a short-cut. Your diary is a good place for lists because in a list you can shape and organize your thoughts without having to write complete sentences.

Saturday, January 17, 1992

take books back to library
get a haircut
finish science project
remind Mom I need sneakers!

When you are in a hurry or are too tired to write a long entry in your journal, take a shortcut and simply list everything that happened in the day.

new kid in class—Jake I forget his last name
blue sweat shirt stolen in gym
found a quarter in the locker room
played handball with Donnie and Kareem

Keep a list of the movies you see and the tapes you have. List the books you've read and what you thought about them. When you list a favorite book, think what makes it so special. Is there a character you like? Did the ending make you feel good? Does a certain scene stand out in your mind?

List ten things you hate, then ten things you love.

> I HATE liver, runny eggs, sour milk, lumps in my mashed potatoes, Mom's face when she's mad, war, throwing up, mean teachers . . .

> I LOVE french fries, my dog, Oreos, sunny days, the Mets, peanut butter, no school, soccer, the beach, ME . . .

List the qualities you like about yourself. (Louisa May Alcott, the author of *Little Women,* called them virtues.) List what you don't like about yourself. If you have thought of many more qualities you don't like, think hard about what you can add to your list of "virtues."

> *Fruitlands*
> *Massachusetts, 1845*

> "What virtues do you wish more of?" asks Mr. Lane, my teacher. I answer:

> Patience
> Obedience
> Industry
> Love and Generosity
> Respect

Silence
Perseverance
Self-Denial

"What vices less of?"

Idleness
Impatience
Selfishness
Wilfulness
Impudence
Activity
Vanity
Pride
Love of Cats

LOUISA MAY ALCOTT, age 12
(from *Louisa May Alcott: Her Life, Letters and
Journals*)

Bronxville, New York
October 5, 1945

What I like about myself

1. my long legs
2. the way I can make people laugh
3. my honesty
4. never staying mad long the way Mom
   does

What I dislike about myself

1. my bushy hair
2. getting my feelings hurt, then covering
   up by laughing

3. losing things
4. feeling jealous of Pat

CARLA MCBRIDE, age 14

Carla is the author of this book!

List what you are afraid of:

getting mugged
failing 5th grade
my mom dying
my apartment getting on fire

Most of us are in touch with all our senses only for brief moments each day. Write down what you see and hear and smell. List the smells you love and the smells you hate.

I love the smell of my sneakers,
bacon cooking, grass after it has
been cut, hot tar on the road . . .

I hate the smell of dog doo, garbage
trucks, burnt toast, the bathroom
after Dad has used it . . .

Now think about the sounds that are pleasing to your ears and then the sounds that frighten or irritate you.

the mockingbird's song
waves breaking on the beach

wind rustling the oak leaves
me on the drums

car alarm going off in the night
ambulance sirens
growling dogs
boom box blasting rap music

List every single thing you do in one day and the time it takes to do each thing. Make the same kind of list in another week and on another day. What did you find out about how you spend your time? Are you surprised at how many hours you spend eating and sleeping and watching TV?

If it is hard for you to make up your mind about something you are thinking of doing, list the reasons for and against in your diary.

This is what Sara Stevens wrote one summer when she was trying to make up her mind whether to take a job at a nearby stable.

For	Against
love the horses	have to get up at 5:30 A.M.
can ride much more often	Sam is very bossy
will make some money	mucking out stables is hard work

Sara grew up in Bridgewater, Connecticut. It didn't take her long to decide to accept the job!

Your diary can remind you of the richness of your life even when you are having a hard time. At the end of each day write down one or two things that have brought you pleasure. You will be surprised at what you discover, for it is often brief, unexpected moments that most delight a person.

> Beanie purring in my ear
> catching snowflakes on my tongue
> finding my jackknife in the driveway

List what your diary means to you.

> my secret friend
> a safe place for my dreams
> a way of letting off steam
> a record of what I do each day

To find out what you've avoided in your diary, make a list of all the things you do not write about.

> my mother dying—because it might come true
> feeling dumb most of the time
> being the shortest kid in the class
> my brother getting AIDS
> worries that have no words to describe them

~ 3 ~

From Drawings
to Stories
to Dreams

"What sort of diary should I like mine to be?" the writer Virginia Woolf asks. "I should like it to resemble some deep old desk, or capacious hold-all, in which one flings a mass of odds and ends without looking them through."

Your diary can also contain "a mass of odds and ends" —drawings, dreams, dialogues, letters, poems, lists, and stories. The more you "embrace anything, solemn, slight or beautiful" that comes to your mind, the more interesting your diary will be.

Drawings

An artist uses a sketchbook to make quick drawings of what catches his or her eye—a sleeping cat, a street fair, feet in a subway car, a snow-covered mailbox. You too can use your diary as a sketchbook. Draw your room so that you will always remember what it looks like. Draw your cat because you love her. Draw even if you think you don't know how to draw. No one is going to look over your shoulder and ask, "What's that?"

Draw the way you feel at this very moment. Fresh impressions fade quickly if you do not capture them on paper.

Dialogues

A dialogue is a conversation carried on with someone or something. We engage in a dialogue when we talk with another person, exchanging ideas and opinions.

In your diary, you can make up dialogues or record those that really took place. Dialogues can be funny or sad, real or imaginary. You can have a dialogue with your homework, your dog or cat, mother or father, teacher or best friend.

When you make up a dialogue, you have to put yourself in someone else's shoes. You not only express your own viewpoint but you also have to be aware of how the other person feels. For example, if you have a dialogue with your room, you have to imagine how your room would respond to you if it could talk.

Room: Where have you been? You haven't thought about me all week.

Me: Oh, yes I have. I just haven't had time to pay attention to you.

Room: I'm a mess. Help! I can't even see myself anymore.

Me: I know, I know. I'll pick up so you'll feel better, I promise.

Room: Just how would YOU feel if you looked like me!

Me: I wish you didn't care so much about how you look. Looks aren't everything, you know.

Recording a quarrel that you had with someone can help you to understand why it occurred. Michael Karp was the only boy in a family of four children growing up in Westport, Connecticut. He recorded the following exchange between his father and himself in October, 1974, when he was twelve years old.

I figured out why Dad and I fight so much.

Dad: I want you to rake the yard this morning.

Me: I can't. I've got soccer practice.

Dad: So what does that mean?

Me: (getting angry) It means I can't rake the leaves this morning.

Dad: (looking really mad) Oh yes you can.

Me: No, I can't. I have to be at school by ten.

Dad: When are you going to do some work around here?

Me: I'll do the leaves in the afternoon when I get back.

Dad: See to it that you do or you're going to be off that team.

Me: O.K., O.K.

I wish Dad had said: Those leaves need raking. When do you think you can do them?

Me: I'll try to get started on them this afternoon after practice. If I don't finish I'll rake the rest tomorrow.

But no. He's always turning everything into a test of who's boss.

A dialogue with yourself can sometimes help you to sort through a problem you feel confused about. It can also be useful if you are trying to talk yourself out of a bad habit.

You're eating too much chocolate again.
So what.
Just wait 'til those zits appear on your face!
Who cares.
You do. And you know it.
Well, what if I do?
So throw out the two chocolate bars you bought yesterday.
Are you kidding?
No, I'm not kidding. You'll feel much better about yourself if you do.
I won't eat them. I'll just put them away somewhere.
You know perfectly well that won't work.
I guess you're right. I'll give them to Billy.
That's better!

Letters Never Sent

A diary is a good place to write a letter that you have no intention of sending. Perhaps you want to write down how you feel about someone you really like in your class. Or perhaps you are angry at a member of your family and you know you will feel better if you can let off steam in your diary.

Amsterdam, Holland
Sunday, July 11, 1943

Dear Kitty,
To return to the "upbringing" theme for the umpteenth time, I must tell you that I am really trying to be helpful, friendly, and to do everything I can so that the rain of rebukes dies down to a light summer drizzle. It is mighty difficult to be on such model behavior with people you can't bear, especially when you don't mean a word of it. But I do really see that I get on better by shamming a bit, instead of my old habit of telling everyone exactly what I think (although no one ever asked my opinion or attached the slightest importance to it).

ANNE FRANK, age 13
(from *Anne Frank: The Diary of a Young Girl*)

Perhaps, like Matt, you might even want to write a letter to yourself!

Toms River, New Jersey
June 25, 1990

Dear Me,
Just had to write you a note and tell you that
you were the best hitter on the team again
today. You're really, really good, Matt. Really,
really, good. If you keep it up like you've been
doing, you're gonna be a great ball player. And
I mean it, too. Maybe even make the Mets!!!!!

Good luck!
Your friend, Matt

Matthew O'Grady is nine years old. He has three sisters
and four brothers and they all love to play baseball.

January 10, 1990

Dear Paul,
I wish I could tell you how much I like you but
you would only laugh at me. You think Loretta
is real nice but she isn't. She makes fun of people behind their backs. I'm a much better
friend than she is, only you don't know it.

CHARLAYNE EVANS, age 11

Charlayne lives in San Diego, California. She has just
begun to keep a diary.

Poems

Many published diaries and journals contain poems tucked in among the other entries. For the reader, they are like an unexpected gift.

Marjorie Fleming wrote the following poem in her journal:

Kirkcaldy, Scotland,
1809

EPHIBOL ON MY DEAR LOVE ISABELLA

Here lies sweet Isabell in bed
With a nightcap on her head
Her skin is soft her face is fair
And she has very pretty hair
She and I in bed lies nice
And undisturbed by rats and mice
She is disgusted with Mr Wurgan
though he plays upon the organ
A not of ribans on her head
Her cheak is tinged with conscious red
Her head it rests upon a pilly
And she is not so very silly
Her nails are neat, her teeth are white
her eyes are very very bright
In a conspicuous town she lives
And to the poor her money gives

Here ends sweet Isabellas story
And may it be much to her glory

MARJORIE FLEMING, age 6
(from *Marjorie Fleming*)

Marjorie Fleming was born on January 15, 1803, in the Scottish town of Kirkcaldy. Her teenage cousin, Isabella Keith, became her tutor when she was five and a half years old and encouraged her to keep a journal. Marjorie often used words she heard from adults without knowing their meaning. She even coined a new word—"ephibol."

Marjorie died of measles when she was not quite nine years old. More than fifty years later, a book describing her life and including her wonderful diary and letters was published in England.

Robert Frost, the poet, tells us that "a poem begins as a lump in the throat, a homesickness, a lovesickness. It finds the thought and the thought finds the words." In your diary, poetry can be another way of expressing in words your awareness of what lies around you.

Poems can be written about anything and everything. Some rhyme and others do not. You can write about the flu that kept you a prisoner at home for a week or about the raccoon that was hit by a car in front of your house. You can write about an ice storm in midwinter or the heat of a midsummer's day in the city. All of life is poetry's concern.

There is no right way to begin a poem, but it is better not to plan your ideas in advance. Let yourself be surprised by what you write, and put down everything that occurs to you. Remember that you are writing only to please yourself. William Stafford, another poet, tells us that "to get started I will accept anything that occurs to me. . . . If I put down something, that thing will help the next thing come and I'm off. If I let the process go on, things will occur to me that were not at all in my mind when I started. These things, odd or trivial as they may be, are somehow connected. And if I let them string out, surprising things will happen."

Your best moments are likely to come when your mind opens up and words and images seem to spill out of their own accord.

Kalymnos, Greece
March 24, 1979

Nick got a lamb the other day for Easter. I feel terrible that something as beautiful and sweet has to be killed. Every time I look at the poor thing I get an awful feeling in my stomach. I certainly can stand going without meat in order to save the beast. I wish others had the same feelings. I love animals very much, I feel for them just as I do my human friends.

I wrote this poem thinking about the farm back home. Remembering early morning, 5:00 A.M., the sun coming up, no one else awake except me and all the animals.

The grass tall and brown
The sun rises, burning away the night-time
    chill

I walk, dew seeping into my sandals,
grass tickling my toes
I feel like laughing.

SARA STEVENS, age 15

*When Sara was a teenager, she spent four months work-
ing and studying with a group called Interalp on an island
in Greece. The journal she kept has helped her to recall
vividly that special time in her life.*

Writing from the Inside Out

"Nothing ever happens in my life." "I'm bored. I do the
same old things day in and day out." Yes, there are times
when we all feel that nothing of interest is taking place in
our lives. We want adventure, we look for something exciting and dramatic to happen. This feeling sometimes
spills over into our diaries when we say we have nothing to
write about.

Virginia Woolf, who kept diaries for all of her adult life,
tells us how she thinks about an ordinary day. "Examine
for a moment an ordinary mind on an ordinary day," she
wrote. "The mind receives myriad impressions—trivial,
fantastic, evanescent, or engraved with the sharpness of
steel. From all sides they come, an incessant shower of
innumerable atoms; and as they fall, they shape themselves into the life of Monday or Tuesday. . . ."

It is not what happens in the outside world that is most
important, but the way your imagination works on your
impressions. It matters that you hate your piano lessons,

are afraid of killer bees, love skateboarding, and feel loneliest when you are in a crowd. These are the feelings and impressions that belong in your diary.

Remember that experience is unlimited. It is your imagination that can transform even the most insignificant, "boring" moments of your life into rich source material for stories and poems.

The Mill, the Cotswolds, England
February 2, 1981

There is still wind today but the greyness is interspersed with flashing bouts of moving sunshine. It is exciting weather.

Wind Walking

Weaving in ploughed fields and pasture,
the dark settles,
and I am being made to walk too fast
over bleached bones and feathers.
I let myself fall back,
let the currents which rasp the hills,
shoot the trees and caress the hedges,
wrap around me, blow my face
and lick my eyes.
My body is forgotten and I am soaring.

SEBASTIAN LOUSADA, age 18

Although Sebastian was born and grew up in London, his love of nature was nurtured by the weekends and summers spent at his family's country house in the Cotswolds.

He wrote many poems in the diary he kept when he was a teenager. Today he lives in Vermont and raises parrots!

Stories

A diary can also be a place to jot down ideas for stories, as well as story outlines and drafts. Sometimes stories almost tell themselves, and you write them down as fast as possible. Other times, a story may remain hidden inside you until the right character appears in your mind to tell it. You notice a young girl standing at the bus stop with a suitcase in each hand. Where is she going, and why does she look so sad? Without your imagination, a story might never emerge from what you have just seen.

You wake up in the morning and you hear a steady tapping noise. Where is it coming from? Who is making that noise? Is someone trying to get in touch with you? You go to the window and look out. You see a blue jay breaking open sunflower seeds with his beak on the gutter of the roof. But before you discover the source of the noise, you have written a scary story in your head. Don't let ideas for stories escape completely from your mind. Write them down in your diary.

Family Stories

Family stories are like legends, linking one generation to another. In every family there is at least one wonderful storyteller. Perhaps it is your grandmother. She loves to tell about the time your mother ran away from home when she was eight because she was afraid of being punished for losing her brand-new jacket at school.

Or perhaps it is your grandfather who tells how he came alone from Italy to this country when he was only ten years old to live with his uncle after his parents died. Such stories are repeated and passed on to you and your brothers and sisters. You in turn will pass them, as well as your own stories, on to future generations. By recording them in your journal, you keep these stories alive.

You can also help family members tell new stories by asking them questions. For example, to get your father started you might ask him to tell you about his very worst day in school. Or you might ask him if he ever got into trouble when he was your age. Use your journal for note taking. Then later, write down some of the stories you liked best.

Dreams

Some dreams present us with pleasant surprises when we least expect them. They linger after we awaken, making us feel as if we are still in that unexpected place. Other dreams frighten us. When we wake up, we are relieved to find ourselves safe and sound in our own beds.

Most dreams fade quickly. If your dreams interest you, keep a pad and pencil near your bed so that you can record what you remember of them in your diary. The more you pay attention to your dreams, the more they will surface in your memory. Sometimes writing down a scary dream can help you understand what frightened you. A dream down on paper is not so scary after all.

January 21, 1873

I wonder if those who keep a diary ever record their dreams? For I would like to write about a strange dream I had last night that I cannot put out of my mind.

I dreamed last night that I lay on the pretty white sofa in the nursery, when I saw, sitting above me on the arm of the sofa, a filthy, repulsive girl. She tossed her head so that the tufts of matted hair flew in every direction . . . Then she crept in under the bedcovers, where she quickly became as small and narrow as an earthworm. Before I knew what she meant to do she had crawled into my ear. It was such a horrible sensation having a long worm crawling around in my head that I awoke.

Selma Lagerlöf, age 14
(from *The Diary of Selma Lagerlöf*)

Selma Lagerlöf was born in Sweden in 1858. She became a writer when she grew up. Her books about a little boy called Nils who changes into an elf and sets forth on adventures on the back of a wild goose are still read by children today.

Toms River, New Jersey
August 1, 1990

Last night I dreamt that me and Freddie found a big cave in the woods behind Mac's farm and we went in and then we heard some growling and there was a bear staring at us and he said get out of my house this minut so we did and we ran all the way back to the barn and then I woke up.

MATT O'GRADY, age 9

~ 4 ~

The Power
of Words

Warming Up

It takes imagination to discover fresh and interesting
diary material in the day-to-day happenings of your life.
Some days you may feel stuck about what to write. Like
athletes who do warm-up exercises before they begin to
play a game, you may want to "warm up" with an exercise
before you begin to write about the events of your day.

Use an egg timer or your watch to set a time limit of two
to three minutes. (You can increase it later.) Now write
the first word that comes to your mind—then the next,
and the one after that, as quickly as you can, until a free
flow of words spills out of you like a waterfall.

Write anything that comes into your head until the time
is up. Don't worry about punctuation, spelling, or grammar. The important thing is to keep writing even if you
have to repeat the same word over and over—you'll get

unstuck if you keep going. Don't let anything slow your thoughts, and try not to be critical of what you are writing down.

When the time is up, reread what you have written. Are you surprised by some thoughts and impressions that seemed to come from nowhere? Steve Warren tried this exercise in his creative writing class.

New York City
November 21, 1990

test hard hard sick in my stomach sick and tired of studying why am i doing it i am doing it for my father did you do your homework did you do your homework did you did you did you broken record yeah did you yeah why don't you trust me to do what i have to do wish i could fly away just seth and me and darryl and nick driving west in a caddy free birds are free not me ive never been free not me got to get my parents off my back back up the car shift into first and zoom we're off the bell rang i have to stop

STEVE WARREN, age 16

The egg timer exercise can be interesting and fun to do with a friend, especially if you both begin with the same word. Elizabeth and her friend Tanya started with the word *red* and wrote for one minute. Notice how their thoughts spread in different directions.

Elizabeth's exercise:

red bed sky night sailor's delight red nose red nose dripping from a cold red ribbon Xmas presents my new watch vacation August hot like red peppers sweat sweet I scream you scream we all scream for ice cream

Tanya's exercise:

red blood cut bike car alone lonely tapes singing guitar strings kite fly sky the 4th of July fireworks picnic on the beach lobster red Greg on his surf board my bikini

Feelings into Words

Experience comes to us through our senses. We *see* the snow illuminated by the street lamp, swirling down onto the sidewalk; we *hear* the siren of an ambulance; we *feel* the cold through the windowpane, and imagine the homeless man sleeping in his cardboard box in front of the video store.

Your images and sense impressions linger and become more vivid with your choice of words. It is not necessary to use complex or obscure words; simple, concrete words are often the best.

Susan Magoffin was eighteen when she traveled west on the Santa Fe Trail in 1846. This excerpt from her diary describes both the circumstances of her distress and her feelings about the swarm of mosquitoes that attacked her carriage.

Mud Creek
June 27, 1846

Millions upon millions were swarming around me, and their knocking against the carriage reminded me of a hard rain ... Magoffin came to the carriage and told me to run if I could, with my shawl, bonnet and shoes on (and without opening my mouth, Jane said, for they would choke me) straight to bed. When I got there they pushed me straight under the musquito bar, which had been tied up in some kind of fashion, and oh, dear, what a relief it was to breathe again. There I sat in my cage [tent], like an imprisoned creature frightened half to death.

SUSAN MAGOFFIN, age 18
(from *Down the Santa Fe Trail into Mexico*)

Everyone uses words such as *good, bad, happy, beautiful,* because they offer a quick, effective way to express a feeling or to describe an experience. But if, like Susan Magoffin, you want to keep your impressions from fading away, you will want to be more specific.

"Today's gym class was awful." If Christianne Deschamps had written only that one sentence in her diary, she would have left out the real feelings she had on that day. But she continued:

Urbana, Illinois
January 17, 1977

I started crying and got very depressed because people chose teams and I was almost the last to be picked. A very small thing to upset me but just goes to show how unliked I am.

CHRISTIANNE DESCHAMPS, age 15

Christianne was born in New York City but moved to Urbana, Illinois, when she was a little girl. She kept a diary until she was twenty.

"I had a terrible time getting to sleep last night," Christopher Pratt wrote in his diary. He went on to explain why.

April 24, 1972

Too many thoughts going through my mind. The house, school, my bike trip. Tim and I had a fight which set the scene for my worries. I was also a little afraid of having bad dreams. I wanted to give my mind a rest but I couldn't. It was being overloaded.

CHRISTOPHER PRATT, age 13

Chris grew up in a small town in Connecticut. Most of the time, he and his brother, Tim, were very good friends.

It is not easy to write about a very painful experience such as the death of someone close to you. Your feelings can be so overwhelming that you don't know how or where to begin. But Sarah Davenport's simple words written more than a hundred and forty years ago still have the power to affect us.

Saturday, June 15, 1850

It rained in the morning but it cleared off about noon. My brother was taken very sick this afternoon about one o'clock. Dr. Teller, Dr. Roberts and a few of our neighbors were assembled here. The doctors could do no good he died a little after three oclock he has not been very well although almost always with red cheeks and playful countenance the Drs. pronounced the disease to be the Croup the funeral will be tomorrow afternoon at one o'clock.

Sunday, June 16, 1850

The funeral of my dear little brother was appointed to be at one o'clock this afternoon at the church. We followed him to the grave and there his earthly remains was laid side by side with my other brother and sister and I alone remain.

Monday, June 17, 1850

Warm and pleasant. O how lonesome it is without Burrell everything seems to be so desolate to me without him I wander from one room to another but I cannot find him . . .

Tuesday, June 18, 1850

I have worked a little and read some. But O how lonesome.

Sunday, June 15, 1851 [a year later]

A cool and beautiful day. I have been to church all day. Father came this afternoon. Mr. Fuller preached this forenoon and Mr. Batchelor this afternoon . . . It is now a year to day since my brother died.

Sarah Davenport was born in 1838 and lived on a farm in New Canaan, Connecticut, all her life. She kept a diary for at least three years of her childhood and may have kept it longer. Many diaries discovered years later among the personal belongings of their owners were simply thrown away by people who placed no value on them.

Your diary is a place for writing about your feelings without fear of scolding or ridicule or exposure. It is a place to reveal your longing for someone who will understand you and your sadness over the loss of someone close to you, like Sarah's loss of her brother.

It is also a place for your dreams of growing up to be brave, smart, kind, funny, rich, and just plain terrific!

Monday, March 7, 1977

I kissed a boy for the first time in my life. 2 boys! It was just their job in the play but for me it was ecstacy. If only I had a boyfriend who really WANTED to kiss me. They liked being kissed by Nancy. She's so pretty and feminine. She's like a little bird fluttering across the stage. I feel like a hag. I've been confused so many times with a boy. I wish I was pretty and feminine. I wish I drove the boys wild.

ABBY KESSLER, age 13

No matter what you write or how you write, the very process of writing will help you to accept the validity of your feelings and to seek solutions to the problems you face.

Using a Thesaurus

The longer you keep your diary, the more you will begin to look for new ways to capture and convey your impressions on paper. If you seem to be using the same words again and again to describe what you see and feel, you might want to look at a thesaurus.

The word *thesaurus* comes from the Latin word meaning "treasury" or "storehouse of knowledge." Like a dictionary, it is a book of words. But it also includes their synonyms—that is, words that have the same or nearly the same meaning.

The following is a list of synonyms for the word *crazy:*

> out of one's head, mad, insane, demented, deranged, crazed, touched, out of one's senses, non compos mentis, unhinged, unbalanced, maniacal, delirious, cracked, daft, moonstruck, stark raving mad, disordered, brainsick.

If you were looking for an alternative to the word *crazy,* you would sift through all those synonyms until you found one that you thought appropriate.

Finding the right words to express your thoughts more precisely is not always easy. But the more you write, the more easily words will come to you. Tune in to the way your friends use words. Can you tell when they are having trouble saying what they mean?

When you read, take note of new and interesting words that the author uses to tell his or her story. Are they words that you might find useful? If so, put them in your diary. To help you remember how they were used, perhaps you might even want to copy the sentences in which they appeared.

Metaphors and Similes

Another way to describe more precisely what you see or how you feel is to look for the similarities between two things that are essentially unlike. For example, if you have a stomachache, you might write, "It feels like there's a rat trying to gnaw its way out of my stomach" or, "My stomach is sloshing and churning like our washing machine on the heavy wash cycle."

A comparison between two such dissimilar things tickles our imagination. We take delight in seeing likenesses in unlike things. In the example of your stomachache, you have helped to sharpen our awareness of how awful you feel.

Such comparisons are known as similes. A simile compares two unlike things by linking them with words such as *like, as, as if, resembling,* etc. Abby Kessler described her feelings of boredom in her diary with a simile.

> I feel processed. All my flavor is gone and the world is like a piece of stale bread.

A metaphor also compares two unlike things, but the comparison is implied.

> April and I went out on the lawn to pick dandelions. There were so many—a million gold buttons on a green velvet coat!

Sara Stevens used a metaphor when she described the lawn as "a green velvet coat." In other words, she substituted the figurative words *gold buttons* for the literal word, *dandelions.* When you speak literally you mean exactly what you say. When you use figurative language, however, you create a picture or image (sometimes called a figure of speech) to convey your feeling or idea.

We use metaphors and similes all the time. "My mom is as mad as a wet hen" (simile); "I'm as strong as an ox" (simile); "Gramps says I have a heart of gold" (metaphor); "It's raining cats and dogs" (metaphor). In fact, we use some metaphors and similes so often they have lost their freshness.

The most meaningful metaphors and similes are those that will surface unexpectedly as you write in your journal. They seem to come from deep within, when your thoughts and feelings are so intense that you feel compelled to try to describe them. Often they come to you when you are most sharply aware of the world around you.

Words have enormous power. They connect us to Sarah's grief at the death of her little brother. They enable us to share Susan's fright at being attacked by a swarm of mosquitoes, and Abby's joy over her first kiss.

Although words can never become more than a commentary on your feelings or your experiences, you can see your thoughts take shape and grow as you write in your diary. Words help awaken us to ourselves.

~ 5 ~

The World Observed

Traveling With Your Diary

If you are going to take a long or special trip, you may want to keep a separate diary. A good travel journal relies on your powers of observation and on your ability to reflect on new experiences. You become more alert to sensations, sights, and sounds when you write about them because you are deliberately trying to convey the uniqueness of each day. Even a visit to a grandparent can be turned into a voyage of discovery if you are willing to put up with the boredom that sometimes accompanies going from one familiar place to another.

A hundred years ago, it was not unusual for families of wealth and privilege to travel abroad for long periods of time. It was considered to be of much greater educational value than going to school. One evening in 1868, Theodore Roosevelt's father, Theodore Roosevelt, Sr., sat down and made an itinerary for a family trip that would cover nine countries and take a year.

Teedie (as he was called then) and his brother and two sisters didn't like the idea but they had nothing to say about it. So on May 12, 1869, the Roosevelts left New York and ten days later they landed in Liverpool, England.

New York City
May 12, 1869

We go to Europe today. We sail in the English Steamship, Scotia. It was verry hard parting from our friend. Old Grand Papa came up to us. While going to the docks I cried a great deal.

THEODORE ROOSEVELT, age 10

Teedie was a poor speller but that did not stop him from writing in great detail about where they went and what they saw. Almost every day the Roosevelt family did what all good tourists do—visited places of historic interest.

London
July 10, 1869

We all went to the tower of London. A kind man dressed like an ancient warden showed us round and we saw a shield made of croci-diles back, all the prisons, and Saxon, Norman, Irish, Roman, Greek, Welsh, and even Chinese armour and weapons. We saw horse armour and foot armour, pike men and archers and I put my head on the block where so maney had been beheaded. We drove and saw the Princess of Wales.

THEODORE ROOSEVELT, age 10

But there was also opportunity for wild play with his brother, Elliott, and his sister, Corinne, and he included those times in his diary as well.

Genoa, Italy
December 10, 1869

Ellie [Elliott] and I went and changed some common centimes [money] for rare ones. Then—but before I go on I must tell you what a play we had in bed early this morning. It was dark as pitch when Ellie and I began to jump. This woke Connie [Corinne]. She came in. We got noisy. We jumped about pulled the covering off the bed and kicked and made an offul noise. Then Father came in and made us quiet.

THEODORE ROOSEVELT, age 11

Teedie was homesick much of the time and he was often physically ill with asthma attacks. But in spite of these troubles, he never missed writing about a single one of the 377 days he was away except for the stormy week while on the boat returning home!

In those days, cameras were so large and heavy that no

one would even think of taking one along on a trip. Today, however, a camera is an indispensable part of travel for most people. Later, the pictures taken will provide a good visual record, especially if each photograph is accompanied by a written caption describing what it shows and the date.

Photographs are not a substitute for the entries you make in your journal, though. Months later, after you have returned home and your memories of the trip have begun to fade, reread your travel journal. You will discover that your description of a special moment is probably more vivid and interesting than all the photographs of the places you and your family visited that day.

Teedie and his family climbed to the top of Mount Vesuvius, the volcano that buried the ancient city of Pompeii.

Naples, Italy
December 31, 1869

I put my hand into a strap that a man had and I began the ascent of the snow covered Mt. Vesuvius . . . I got up to a wall inside of which there came steam that warmed me. The rest at last came up. We all warmed ourselves and then went on. The sulpher smoke now came sweeping down on us in places and made me breathe short. At last we came to a hole rather bigger than my arm round which the smoke came blindingly.

Looking down this hole you saw a red flame and heard a roaring. This was a small crater. I put my Alpine stick in and it caught fire right away. I took it out and it went out immediately but is all black. The smoke was to much for Ellie and Conie who did not go. We went to a bigger crater where pushing down some small pebbles they instantly flew up in our faces. . . .

THEODORE ROOSEVELT, age 11
(from *The Roosevelt Diaries of Boyhood and Youth*)

Teedie's diary entries were less long and detailed when he returned but he continued to keep a diary for the next thirty years. When he grew up, he became President of the United States. As President, he made conservation a popular cause. He increased the area of our National Forests by forty million acres, established five National Parks, sixteen National Monuments (including the Grand Canyon), and fifty-one National Bird Sanctuaries. He also wrote more than twenty books dealing with history, natural history, and politics!

The fun of traveling lies not only in the freshness and excitement of new experiences but also in the surprises that come to you when fragments of your past return to you in a memory. A certain campsite or motel, someone you see in a restaurant or on the street, may remind you of a place you have been to before or of a close friend. Sometimes an unfamiliar place may even make you feel homesick for your comfortable, familiar life back home.

Uganda, Africa
February 10, 1972

The Parra is a blah structure which may not be so bad since it is surrounded with animals and all the rooms look out over the Nile. Elephants visit regularly and the Marabu storks herd over the garbage pit while the vultures wait patiently above. . . . Its a bird watchers paradise, kingfishers, herons, egrets, storks, eagles, sandpipers, cormorants everything. I just heard a hippo roar, it sounds like a giant bull frog. I am sick and tired of hanging around the old fogies. I hope my friends will treat me in the same way when I get back as they did before I left. I think they will have changed much more than I have.

CHRISTOPHER PRATT, age 13

Christopher Pratt was thirteen years old when he and his family took a year-long trip around the world. During that time he kept a diary and wrote about the places he visited and the people he met. He recorded not only what he saw but what he felt at the time, too.

Rhodesia, Africa
February 22, 1972

When I first got a look at Victoria Falls, I was impressed but slightly disappointed. As we moved on to the next vantage point, the view became more spectacular and then the next was better until we were facing the main falls, a continual avalanche, snow white, and booming sheets of water. It's a violent place, water coming down, water spraying up, rain coming down and sun. A rainbow stretching its semi-circular arch across the great ravine to which the Zambia River plummets. The spray causes a rain forest getting a continual rain. I remember distinctly when I was in 6th grade studying about Victoria Falls. I was very interested in the rain forest.

CHRISTOPHER PRATT, age 13

Wherever you go—on a canoe trip, to a friend's house overnight, or to a faraway place like Africa—you carry along your own unique history created from everything you have experienced in your life thus far. And when you return home, you bring back something from the unfamiliar place that will remain in your memory forever.

Chicago, Illinois
1869

Europe is a dream, while hotels, bad eating, and sea-sickness are things of the past. I know it won't last but a few months, nevertheless I am home, yes actually home. Here I am in the old house where I was born and where I wish I could always live. It is the dearest place on earth to me and worth all London, Paris and

New York put together. They may say what
they like, still I shall persist in my opinion, that
there is no place equal to Chicago, and no
place like home.

JULIA NEWBERRY, age 14
(from *Julia Newberry's Diary*)

*At the same time Theodore Roosevelt was traveling
through Europe, Julia was just returning from a similar
trip. She was four years older than Teedie and her observations were also very detailed, though she spent more
time describing the dinner parties and fancy balls that she
attended. Like Teedie, she was often homesick. Her diary
was discovered in an old chest more than fifty years after
her death. She died in Italy when she was just twenty-two
years old.*

Remember to date each of the entries in your travel
diary, and be sure to include the names of people you met
and places you visited. You may think you will remember
everything because each experience is so new to you at
the time, but too soon after you return home, you discover
that one face or place blends into another.

Tape mementoes in your diary—a menu, a map, for-
eign money, postcards, tickets to special events—anything that will help to refresh your memory of the trip.
And don't forget to make a quick sketch of something that
especially catches your eye!

There is an old Chinese proverb that says, "The palest
ink is clearer than the sharpest memory." Someday those
few words you scribbled in your diary in haste, and the

sketch you made to accompany them, will be enough to bring back the excitement you felt over seeing something new and different for the first time.

Observing Nature in Your Journal

You don't have to travel far to experience the joys of discovery, for all kinds of activity take place in your own front and back yard—even in your bedroom! Have you ever tried to guess which raindrop will win the race down your windowpane? Or watched a fly struggling to escape from a spiderweb? Use your powers of observation to record in your diary the day-to-day happenings in the natural world that surrounds you.

Suffolk, England
September 28, 1833

I found a honeysuckle leaf rolled up in a curious way by means of a gummy substance, and 6 or 7 beautiful lady-birds [ladybugs] comfortably lodged within it. I suppose it is their nest.

EMILY SHORE, age 14

Woodbury, England
July 20, 1835

For two or three days I have observed a species of wasp come frequently into my room, and enter the keyhole of my dressing-table drawer, where it stayed a considerable time.

This morning, I found two green caterpillars in the lock, each rolled up in a particular position, and both alive. It did not occur to me that there was any connection between their appearance and the visits of the wasp, and I was much puzzled to account for their being there. Soon after, the wasp returned, bearing, to my surprise, one of these caterpillars amongst its feet. I then discovered that it was the *Odynerus muscarius,* or mason wasp, which always hoards up caterpillars in its nest for its progeny to eat; and I was greatly pleased at the opportunity of watching its curious habits.

EMILY SHORE, age 16
(from *The Journal of Emily Shore*)

Emily Shore was born in 1819 at Woodbury and spent all her life at home. She never went to school but was educated by her parents. She lived in two worlds—the world of nature and the world of her imagination. She collected plants, studied the habits of birds and insects, and wrote plays and stories. She kept a journal beginning July 5, 1831, when she was twelve years old and ending June 24, 1839, two weeks before she died of tuberculosis at age nineteen and a half.

We know so much more about the world than Emily Shore did more than a hundred and fifty years ago. Today we can turn to a wide variety of books, television programs, films, tapes, and videos for information. But these

resources cannot take the place of our direct, active observation of the natural world.

Devon, England
August 15, 1905

A hot, sultry afternoon, during most of which
I was stretched out on the grass beside an up-
turned stone where a battle royal was fought
between Yellow and Black Ants. The victory
went to the hardy little Yellows. . . . By the way,
I held a Newt by the tail today and it emitted
a squeak! So the Newt has a voice after all.

BARBELLION, age 15
(from *The Journal of a Disappointed Man*)

Barbellion's real name, as you may remember, was Bruce
Frederick Cummings. Although he became a biologist
when he grew up, he is best known for his diary.

Taking notes on your observations of the natural world
can help to set you in the direction of becoming a natural
scientist when you grow up. Examining the ways insects
and animals live their lives will make you aware of aspects
of their behavior that still need to be explained. Your observations might even lead to a new discovery, for this is
just how such discoveries are made!

One spring day in 1982, Sebastian Lousada saw a young
buzzard in a pet shop in London and bought it. He kept a
detailed journal of his experiences training this young
hawk while living alone in an old mill house in the Cots-

wolds. Sebastian's journal ends after the bird, having learned to catch her own food and fly, is set free to live in the wild.

The Mill, the Cotswolds, England
March 3, 1982

The bird was good again today and she came about nine feet. Her first attempt was another disaster though. Her jesses [leather straps attached to her legs] got caught around the post somehow and as she took off, she also fell—a kind of undignified bate* if bates can ever be dignified. I apologized to her and gave her a piece of meat to compensate. After a while, she calmed down again. She stares at me and crouches sleekly before she lifts those tattered wings and flies toward me. It is exciting to watch her although not as thrilling as seeing the flashing kestrel move by, wild and free.

SEBASTIAN LOUSADA, age 18

Bate means "to flutter wildly from fist or perch."

Do you have to have special knowledge to keep a "nature" diary? No, but you have to be observant and patient and not easily bored. Above all, you need to be curious about plants and animals in their natural environment.

Examine a fly, a spiderweb, an ant, a moth. Draw them in your diary.

Record your observations of the weather each day.

Look for pigeons' nests on the ledges of buildings and list the birds that frequent your back yard.

Start a sweet potato plant from an "eye," an avocado plant from a seed. Describe how they grow.

Observe, then record what you observe in your journal. Your ideas about the world will change as you see and learn more. What you will gain is a profound awareness of the endless diversity of life. And the discoveries you make on your own will stay in your mind forever.

~ 6 ~

From Diaries to Books

After keeping your journal for a while, you may discover how much you enjoy writing. You may even think that you would like to become a writer when you grow up. Most writers, at one time or another, have kept diaries or notebooks in which they stored notes and random observations. Some have turned to their early diaries as a source of ideas for their creative work.

Elwyn Brooks White, better known as E. B. White, the author of *Stuart Little, Charlotte's Web,* and *The Trumpet of the Swan,* began to keep a journal when he was eight years old. He made daily entries until he was twenty-eight. He didn't spend much time describing day-to-day events. Instead he wrote about his relationships with his parents and friends, his fears, and his shyness.

He also wrote stories and poems and sent them to a magazine popular at the time called *St. Nicholas.* When Elwyn was eleven years old he won a silver medal for a dog story and three years later he won a gold medal for another dog story. He loved animals of all kinds and he learned about them by observing them.

It is possible that young Elwyn decided to keep a journal because he wanted to become a writer, and he knew that the discipline of writing something every day would ultimately be a help to him. Much later, when he wrote *The Trumpet of the Swan,* he turned to his early diaries for ideas about how an eleven-year-old thinks about life. In the book, Sam worries about how to be honest with his father and still maintain his independence, just as Elwyn White did when he was the same age.

There are no excerpts from his diaries in this book because the diaries were never published. In fact, he requested that his diaries be destroyed after his death.

Three other young diarists—Wanda Gág, Beatrix Potter, and Louisa May Alcott—whose diaries have been published, all became writers of books for children. Wanda Gág, who shared her resolutions with us earlier, believed that keeping a diary when she was a young teenager gave her courage later to explore her ideas in story and picture book form. When she grew up, she wrote and illustrated *Millions of Cats* and *The Funny Thing* and *Snippy and Snappy,* books still read and loved by children around the world.

Wanda began keeping a diary when she was fifteen. She carried a notebook wherever she went and she always tried to get things down: "sometimes an immediate recording of an episode or conversation or of my thoughts and emotions. Since my pen was always racing with my thoughts, the writing is scribble and often all but illegible."

Wanda Gág was born in New Ulm, Minnesota, in 1893, the eldest of eight children. Her father was an artist who decorated houses and churches, so he encouraged everyone in the family to draw and to write stories and poems. When Wanda was fifteen, her father died, leaving his family only the house they lived in and a thousand dollars in insurance. Her mother's health was very poor, so Wanda was expected to leave school to help support the family.

Wanda was determined that she and her brothers and sisters would finish high school. She sold drawings, poems, and stories to newspapers and gave drawing lessons to children to supplement the family's meager income. All the while, she wrote regularly in her diary.

Wednesday, December 15, 1908

Poor Diary, how did you feel being left up here at school two nights and a day? I needed you badly last Monday, I was so cross and exasperated I nearly cried, and it would have done me good to write my troubles in here and drop them from my mind after that.

Yesterday was Tuesday and I stayed home from school because—well, I may as well say the reason—I didn't have a decent dress to wear. Those happy rags of mine!

Saturday, January 8, 1909

Read over some of the stories I wrote last year in English Composition. There's one sentimental one about a flower which is simply awful, and another one about a dog which is awfully simple. I guess nearly all of my stories belong to either of these two classes.

WANDA GÁG, age 15
(from *Growing Pains*)

Wanda kept her journal for over thirty years. She filled thirty-one notebooks "with diagrams, self portraits, and other sketches, with many crossed-out words in spots and even tear blots." Years later, excerpts from Wanda's diaries were published in a book called *Growing Pains*, an appropriate title for this record of the joys and sorrows of an honest, self-searching young person. In addition to writing and illustrating her wonderful children's books, Wanda drew and painted pictures and made woodcuts, etchings, and lithographs. Her work can still be found in some museums and art galleries throughout the United States.

Louisa May Alcott, the author of *Little Women*, was born on November 29, 1832, sixty-one years before Wanda's birth. Like Wanda, Louisa was very poor while she was growing up, but her family's poverty was the result of her father's high ideals. Amos Bronson Alcott was a philosopher and a teacher. Unfortunately, his students, though they were devoted to him, were unable to contribute much money toward the support of the Alcott family.

Louisa began keeping a diary when she was seven years old. She and her sisters did not go to school. Instead, they were tutored at home by their parents. Louisa and her three sisters were required to keep journals as part of their education, and their parents read them and wrote comments in them from time to time. This did not seem to inhibit Louisa. In fact, it may have encouraged her to write more.

When her father looked over Louisa's journals, he concluded that while her older sister Anna's journal "was about other people, Louisa's journal was about herself." Louisa agreed. "That is true, for I don't talk about myself. Yet must always think of the wilful, moody girl I try to manage in my journal. I write of her to see how she gets on."

Thursday, January 29, 1843

It was Father's and my birthday. We had some nice presents. We played in the snow before school. Mother read "Rosamond" when we sewed. Father asked us in the eve what fault troubled us most. I said my bad temper. I told Mother I liked to have her write in my book. She said she would put in more and she wrote this to help me: Dear Louy, your handwriting improves very fast. Take pains and do not be in a hurry. I like to have you make observations about our conversations and your own thoughts. It helps you to express them and to understand your little self. Remember dear girl that a diary should be an epitome of your life. May it be a record of pure thought and good actions, then you will indeed be the precious child of your loving mother.

LOUISA MAY ALCOTT, age 10

Louisa wrote very little about the poverty she and her sisters faced daily, but her diary is full of her efforts toward self-improvement. Her model was her mother, who remained brave and loving and loyal to her husband and family throughout all their struggles.

Fruitlands, Massachusetts
September 1, 1843

We had bread and fruit for dinner. I read and walked and played till supper-time. We sung in the even. As I went to bed the moon came up very brightly and looked at me. I felt sad because I have been cross today and did not mind Mother. I cried and then I felt better and said that piece from Mrs. Sigourney. "I must not tease my mother." I got to sleep saying poetry. I know a great deal.

LOUISA MAY ALCOTT, age 10
(from *Louisa May Alcott: Her Life, Letters and Journals*)

When Louisa was ten, the Alcotts and some friends who shared Mr. Alcott's beliefs bought a farm not far from Concord, Massachusetts, and named it Fruitlands. It was to be an experiment in living together. Louisa's father had very definite ideas about the best way to live and how children should be educated. He believed that education should be pleasant and interesting, not a chore. When children learned about nature, for example, he believed that they should learn in nature's laboratory, the out-of-doors. He encouraged his children to be imaginative—to paint and write and make up plays. Today, his ideas don't seem so strange, but a hundred and fifty years ago, they were considered most unusual.

Mr. Alcott also believed that a vegetable diet would produce "sweetness of temper and disposition." Someone overheard young Louisa say to a friend, "I don't know about that. I've never eaten meat and I'm awful cross and irritable very often." Not only did her father impose a strict vegetarian diet (no fish, eggs, milk, cheese, or butter) but his family were limited to eating only "aspiring vegetables," which meant those that grew above ground. He did not approve of the "degraded" forms that burrow in the earth. That left out potatoes and all the other root vegetables such as carrots, beets, onions, and turnips.

"We had bread and fruit for supper," Louisa often records in her diary. To make matters worse, Mr. Alcott was not a very good farmer. He planted his crops late and carelessly and he was often away lecturing when the vegetables were ready to be harvested. For a while, Louisa and her mother tried to teach sewing to earn a little money, but life for the Alcott family was very hard.

Louisa grew up to become the kind of person she wanted to be—a "truly good and useful woman." When her book *Little Women* was published in 1868, it was a great success. She was able to support her family with the money she earned from its sales.

The story describes the childhood experiences of Jo March and her three sisters, many of which were first recorded in Louisa's early diaries. Jo is really Louisa herself, and one of the first feminist heroines in American fiction. The self-sacrificing Marmee is patterned after

Louisa's own beloved mother, and the three sisters Meg, Amy, and Beth resemble her real sisters. Many years later, Louisa claimed that her early diaries helped give shape to the fiction she wrote when she grew up.

As children, Wanda Gág and Louisa May Alcott were surrounded by their large families. They had almost no moments of quiet and solitude in their young lives. How different Beatrix Potter's life was! The author of *The Tale of Peter Rabbit*, *The Tale of Benjamin Bunny*, and a dozen other stories was born in England in 1866. Unlike Louisa's parents, who encouraged her to join in their discussions, Mr. and Mrs. Potter believed that "children should be seen and not heard." But Beatrix was not even seen very often by her parents. She spent most of her early years in the nursery, rarely going anywhere except for a daily walk with her nurse.

When her brother, Bertram, who was five years younger, went to school, Beatrix remained at home. As she wrote later about her childhood, "It was in the days when parents kept governesses, and only boys went to school in most families." She knew no other children except for a few cousins who occasionally came to tea. Yet, oddly enough, she was not an unhappy child. Even before she was five years old, she was copying pictures of animals and birds from natural history books. All the while, she was observing life around her very closely.

When Beatrix was five years old, her family began going to the North of England for their holidays. It was there in the fields and woods that Beatrix's imagination began to take hold. Later, rabbits appeared in her notebooks wearing scarves and carrying umbrellas.

> I have got my hedgehog with me too. She enjoys going by train. She is always very hungry when she is on a journey. I carry her in a little basket.
>
> Hunca Munca is very much alive; she was caught in a mouse-trap two years ago, and now she is so tame she will sit on my finger. She lives in a cage with another mouse called Apply Dapply.

Even more unusual than Beatrix's isolated childhood is her diary, which she began keeping regularly when she was fourteen. She never spoke of it to anyone. After she died in 1952, her relatives found among her possessions a large bundle of loose pages and exercise books all filled with a mysterious code. She did not leave a key to the code, probably because she didn't want anyone to read her journals. In fact, she wrote on one page, "No one will ever read this."

After trying unsuccessfully to decipher the code, relatives asked a friend, Leslie Linder, for help. Linder worked on the code for a year, also without success. He was about to give up when he noticed a line at the bottom of a page that contained the Roman numeral XVI and the Arabic number 1793. Could that be the year 1793, perhaps? And did the Roman numerals belong to a king or queen?

Linder tried to find out what important events took place that year. He discovered that the French king, Louis XVI, was beheaded in Paris in 1793. Returning to Beatrix's journal, Linder saw a word in that same sentence containing the letter X. He guessed that the word might be *executed*. With the help of these few symbols, he eventually deciphered the code. The sentence containing that Roman numeral read: "An old woman was buried at Paris last Saturday aged 107 who was present at the execution of Louis XVI in 1793."

Beatrix wrote in ink on single and folded sheets of notepaper. When she was fifteen her code writing was comparatively large. A year later her handwriting grew smaller, and the year following, her writing became extremely small, with more symbols joined together. A sheet about the size of this page contained more than fifteen hundred words on only one side!

Here is Beatrix's code alphabet:

a	a	**ђ**	k	**ʊ**	u
ι	b	**t**	l	**η**	v
ꝛ	c	**n**	m	**m**	w
ꝍ	d	**m**	n	**x**	x
k	e	**e**	o	**η**	y
c	f	**ꝑ**	p	**ʒ**	z
ꝝ	g	**q**	q	**2**	to, too, two
ι	h	**ω**	r	**3**	the, three
ι	i	**γ**	s	**4**	for, four
ι	j	**1**	t	**✝**	and

You can see that although she included some of the letters of our alphabet, most stood for different letters.

She also used some characters from the Greek alphabet and from German. The rest of the code symbols she made up.

If you read Beatrix's journal today (it is published in book form and is called *The Journal of Beatrix Potter*) you will wonder why she went to so much trouble to keep it a secret. There is none of the self-searching or self-doubting that you can find in Louisa's and Wanda's diaries. Instead, her journal contains detailed descriptions of places she visited and pictures she saw in museums and galleries. She also wrote about the plants and animals she observed in nature, and included curious anecdotes gleaned from newspapers.

Sunday, July 2, 1882

The authorities collect from the streets of Manchester and the dust bins in one year (it is said) seven tons of dead dogs and thirteen of cats. These are boiled down. The oil is worth a good deal, being in great request for making Olio Margarine and other artificial butters!

BEATRIX POTTER, age 16

Sunday, January 27, 1884

There was another story in the paper a week or so since. A gentleman had a favorite cat whom he taught to sit at the dinner-table where it behaved very well. He was in the habit of putting any scraps he left on to the cat's plate. One day puss did not take his place punctually, but presently appeared with two mice, one of which it placed on its master's plate, the other on its own.

BEATRIX POTTER, age 18
(from *The Journal of Beatrix Potter*)

Beatrix kept her secret journal until she was about thirty years old. Then she set it aside because she was becoming more and more involved in writing and illustrating her books for children.

Keeping diaries when they were young has helped many authors to form a habit of writing, a first step toward becoming a writer. But more important, writing helped to awaken their powers of observation. Someday, you too may return to your journals and rediscover the richness of your childhood experiences as a creative source for your own stories and poems.

CHAPTER

~ 7 ~

Sharing a Diarist's Life

While most diaries are not written with the idea that they will be read by strangers, some eventually are published. Often, such diaries come out after the writer's death—Theodore Upson's, Beatrix Potter's, and Anne Frank's are examples. Anaïs Nin and "Helena Morley," on the other hand, were still alive when their diaries became books for others to read.

Historians are particularly interested in old diaries because these records are an important link between the past and the present. They extend our awareness of what it was like to be alive in another time. Often an old diary tells us more about the person who kept the diary than about the great historical events that were taking place in his or her lifetime. Journals kept by soldiers during wars are very interesting to historians because they describe the moment-to-moment experiences of the common soldier.

Both parents of James Madison Doyle died shortly after he was born on May 5, 1845. Jonathan and Elizabeth

Upson, well-to-do farmers living in the nearby town of Lima, Indiana, adopted James and renamed him Theodore Upson. He began to keep a journal when he was thirteen.

Lima, Indiana
March 28, 1858

We have the greatest lot of snow this winter. You can hardly see a fence anywhere. There is a snowdrift in front of our house over 15 feet deep. . . . Us boys have built a big snow fort on the hill north of town and part of them play they are Southerners and the others try to get in and take their slaves. The slaves are not allowed to fight any. When we capture the slaves we send them off to Canada as the Underground Rail Road folks used to do. There has been a big comet this fall and winter. Grandma and some of the old folks say it's a sure sign of war.

THEODORE UPSON, age 13

Theodore was only sixteen when he enlisted in the Union Army. He became a member of the One Hundredth Regiment of Indiana Infantry Volunteers, where he remained throughout the Civil War.

Lima, Indiana
July 6, 1862

We are to go away next week and I am going to write something to leave at home for Father

and Mother to read in case I should never get
back. I am going to leave all that I have written. Mother says she will take care of it for me.
. . . I could never talk to Father about some
things. He always seemed to me to be such a
good man that I could never hope to be anything like as good as he. I know that the one
great fear he has is that after I get into the
Army I will have so many bad influences
around me that I will go to the bad entirely so
I am going to try and write out how I feel and
if I never do return it may be some comfort to
him.

THEODORE UPSON, age 16

Three years later, on June 8, 1865, Theodore was officially
discharged from the army. By the time the war ended, his
regiment had marched four thousand miles and engaged
in twenty-five battles. Out of 937 men, 89 had been killed
in action, 150 died of disease, and an additional 225 had
been discharged because of wounds.

Here is Theodore's account of one of his war experiences.

November 24, 1864

We went down on the line where lay the dead
of the Confederates. It was a terrible sight.
Some one was groaning. We moved a few bod-
ies and there was a boy with a broken arm and
leg—just a boy 14 years old; and beside him,

cold in death, lay his Father, two Brothers, and an Uncle. It was a harvest of death. We brought the poor fellow up to the fire. Our surgeons made him as comfortable as they could. Then we marched away leaving him with his own wounded who we could no longer care for.

THEODORE UPSON, age 18
(from *With Sherman to the Sea*)

After he was discharged, Theodore returned to his parents in Lima, where he spent the rest of his life. He died in 1919 at the age of seventy-six. His journals and letters about his experiences in the Civil War have been published in a book called *With Sherman to the Sea*.

A good diary makes us feel that we are there sharing the diarist's life with him or her. It is almost as if history has been turned inside out. Instead of ordinary people being in the background of great historical events, we see great events such as the Civil War through the eyes of an ordinary person—a young soldier like Theodore Upson.

Earlier in this book, you read an excerpt written by a young girl who called her diary "Kitty." Her name was Anne Frank. She was not famous when she was alive and, in fact, never imagined that one day her diary would become a moving record of the plight of the Jewish people during the World War II Holocaust.

Anne was born in Frankfurt, Germany, in 1929. When she was four years old, her family left Germany because the German leader, Adolf Hitler, had begun to persecute the Jews . . . and the Franks were Jewish. They moved to Amsterdam, Holland, and for a number of years they lived happily there. Then on May 10, 1940, the Nazis invaded Holland and immediately put anti-Jewish laws into effect in that country, too.

Anne received a diary on Friday, June 12, 1942, for her thirteenth birthday.

> Soon after seven I went to Mummy and Daddy and then to the sitting room to undo my presents. The first to greet me was you, possibly the nicest of all.

A week later, on Saturday, June 22, 1942, she wrote:

> I haven't written for a few days because I wanted first to think about my diary. It's an odd idea for someone like me to keep a diary; not only because I have never done so before, but because it seems to me that neither I— nor for that matter anyone else—will be interested in the unbosomings of a thirteen year old school girl. Still, what does that matter? I want to write, but more than that, I want to bring out all kinds of things that lie buried deep in my heart.

In that same diary entry she also wrote:

> Jews must hand in their bicycles. Jews are banned from trains and are forbidden to drive.

Jews are only allowed to do their shopping between 3 and 5 o'clock and then only in shops
which bear the placard "Jewish Shop." Jews
are forbidden to visit theaters, cinemas, and
other places of entertainment. . . . So we were
forbidden to do this and forbidden to do that.
But life went on in spite of it all.

ANNE FRANK, age 13

Anne's father knew that it was only a matter of time
before they would be arrested. The Franks and another
family, the Van Daans, prepared to hide in a "secret
annex" above a warehouse in Amsterdam.

Wednesday, July 8, 1942

Margot and I began to pack some of our most
vital belongings into a school satchel. The first
thing I put in was this diary, then hair curlers,
handkerchiefs, schoolbooks, a comb, old letters; I put in the craziest things with the idea
that we were going into hiding. But I'm not
sorry, memories mean more to me than
dresses.

ANNE FRANK, age 13
(from *Anne Frank: The Diary of a Young Girl*)

Loyal friends who worked during the day in the offices
below the attic brought them food and other necessities.
They also brought news of the terrible war that was being
fought in Europe. Eight people, including Anne, re-

mained hidden in the secret annex for two years. Then one day the Nazis invaded their hiding place and took them all away.

Of the eight people who had lived together, only Mr. Frank survived. Anne died in the concentration camp at Bergen-Belsen, Germany, in 1945. She was not yet sixteen years old.

After the war ended, Anne's father returned to Amsterdam. Dutch friends who had helped him when he and his family were hiding gave Mr. Frank the notebooks and papers they had found on the floor of the attic after the Nazis left. Among these papers was Anne's diary. In letters to her imaginary friend, Kitty, Anne had revealed her deepest feelings—about her parents, about her special friend, Peter, and above all about herself. She was funny and loving and impatient and sad and bored. For two years she described with great honesty the joys and miseries of daily life in that secret hiding place.

Mr. Frank first had copies of Anne's diary printed privately for the remaining friends and members of his family. But they shared it with others who, in turn, urged Mr. Frank to have it published. Today *Anne Frank: The Diary of a Young Girl* is one of the most famous diaries ever published. Translated into thirty-seven languages, it is read by people all over the world.

Anne's diary reminds us that there is a spirit that lies within each of us, a spirit that gives us the courage to remain strong and endure even in the most terrible of circumstances.

"Helena Morley" was born in Brazil in 1881 and grew up in a diamond-mining town called Diamantina. She began to keep a diary when she was twelve years old. When she was sixty-one, she published a small edition of her childhood diary for the amusement of family and friends. It soon became so popular that larger editions were printed and eventually it was translated into English.

"Helena Morley's" real name was Senhora Augusto Mario Caldeira Brant. To maintain her privacy, Senhora Brant chose "Helena" and "Morley" as pseudonyms because they were both names from her father's family. This is what she wrote at the beginning of her book, *The Diary of "Helena Morley,"* to her granddaughters who were the same age she was when she kept the diary:

> You who were born in comfortable circumstances and who feel sorry when you read these stories of my childhood, you do not need to pity poor little girls just because they are poor. We were so happy! Happiness does not consist in worldly goods but in a peaceful home, in family affections, in a simple life without ambition—things that fortune cannot bring and often takes away.

Helena's father, who was a diamond miner, encouraged her to form a habit of writing down everything that happened to her, and that's just what she did. She was good-natured and full of mischief; she and her sister, Luizinha, had fits of giggling (though sometimes Helena was not very nice to Luizinha); and she had lots of friends. She was not a very good student and in fact failed her first year in Normal School, which is the same as high school here in the United States.

Saturday, December 9, 1893

I didn't pass the first year and it was entirely due to bad luck and nothing else. In the geography exam almost all of us cheat. We make concertinas [narrow strips of paper folded like an accordion on which the students write notes]. I went to the exam with my pockets full of them. The subject for the exam turned out to be "Rivers of Brazil." Marvelous! I took out my little concertina and started to copy it, and told the others out loud that they should copy too. I think that's what caught his eye. Senhor Artur Queiroga came down from the platform and stood near my desk and I couldn't possibly go on writing. . . . I had to hand over my concertina and Senhor Artur only asked me to explain why I made that instead of studying. I answered that I didn't know—that that was the way I'd been taught and I thought it was a good system. After this exam others went the same way. The teachers came and distracted me while my schoolmates were peacefully cheating away. It was my bad luck. What can I do?

HELENA MORLEY, age 13
(from *The Diary of "Helena Morley"*)

There was no electricity or running water in the town where Helena grew up, and by our standards today her family was very poor. When we read her diary we find out that she and her sister and brothers took their baths in the local stream, that she had only two or three dresses and two pairs of boots, that she loved sweets, and that she ate cucumbers instead of cereal for breakfast every morning.

Sunday, February 19, 1893

Siá Ritinha, the chicken thief from Cavalhada, spent the whole evening here in the house, telling stories about people who got sick from eating cucumbers, and she finished by saying, "Dona Carolina, you mark my words. The cucumber is so poisonous that if it so much as touches the hem of your skirt, it's dangerous."

During the whole conversation I kept expecting mama to tell her that I won't eat porridge but that I eat two cucumbers with salt every morning. Mama said to me "Do you hear what she's saying? Are you listening?" I wanted to ask Dona Ritinha "And isn't it dangerous to steal your neighbor's chickens?"

HELENA MORLEY, age 13

Helena brings to life her experiences in the small Latin American town of Diamantina at the turn of the century. By the end of her diary, we know her well and wish we could have been her friend.

Some time ago, the artist Eric Sloane found in a New

England attic a diary kept by a fifteen-year-old boy named Noah Blake. (Earlier in this book, we learned how Noah made his diary.) The diary would not be half so interesting to us if it were not for Sloane's drawings and text that enrich our understanding of Noah's way of life in the early nineteenth century. We learn about the way he and his family built their house, how they cured themselves of illness, and what they did to amuse themselves.

Noah kept his diary from his fifteenth birthday on March 25, 1805, to the following Christmas.

> Apr. 9 Flooding all but washed our bridge away. Father says the new bridge beams are seasoned and ready. When the waters subside, he shall begin to erect it. We are shaping the abutments.
>
> Apr. 10 Worked on the bridge abutments. Daniel [the ox] helped with bigger stones.
>
> Apr. 11 Do. [meaning ditto]
>
> Apr. 12 Good Friday. It rained all day.
>
> Apr. 13 Bluebirds arrived. We finished the abutments without the help of Mr. Adams and his son Robert who came by to assist. River lower.
>
> Apr. 14 Easter Sunday. A fine service. Saw Sarah Trowbridge the new girl at the Adams. She is very pretty.
>
> Apr. 22 Day spent in forge barn fashioning trunnels for bridge. Did forty.

(Sloane tells us that trunnels are wooden nails. The Blakes
used them not because they didn't have metal nails but
because metal rusted or split the wood. Wood breathed
with weather changes.)

Apr. 27   The Adams arrived with six towns-
people at sunrise. We set the strings and put
the kingposts in place. We have made a fine
bridge. Father put a bush atop the posts and
we all sang and drank. Sarah brought a cake.
One man fell into the brook but he was not
hurt. We knocked down the old bridge, which
made me feel a little sad.

NOAH BLAKE, age 15
(from *The Diary of an Early American Boy*)

(A small tree or bush tacked on top of a new building
brings good luck. This ancient custom goes all the way
back to a time when people worshiped trees.)

Noah would surely be surprised to discover that his
diary gives readers today a sense of the times in which he
lived as well as a feeling for his character.

Learning about the past is like putting together an
enormous jigsaw puzzle. Each time you discover something new about the way people lived and thought in a
different time, another piece fits into place.

Unlike the diaries of Theodore Upson, Anne Frank,
"Helena Morley," and Noah Blake, many old diaries, logs,
and journals have never been published in book form.

Some, like Sarah Davenport's journal, can be found in your local historical society. Others are tucked away in old boxes or trunks in attics and cellars and remain to be discovered. Perhaps you will be lucky enough to find a diary that someone in your family kept long ago.

And now, what about your own diary? Will one of your great-great-grandchildren discover it among old letters and papers stored in a box or a trunk? If so, imagine their surprise and pleasure when they sit down to read it! For there you will be in its pages—sharing a pizza with your best friend, sick in bed with the flu, hating your visits to the orthodontist, and loving the freedom of school vacations—living your life with honesty and courage.

Diaries act as a mirror—when we read about the experiences of others, we see ourselves more clearly. Almost all the thoughts and feelings in this book seem familiar to us, even though many of them were written by young people who lived in another time. We can imagine what dozens of mosquito bites would feel like; we remember the fun of jumping up and down on our beds and having pillow fights. We too have felt left out and unloved and have had quarrels with a parent or a brother or sister. It's as if the life of each diarist is connected by a common thread that extends over the years to us.

Perhaps someday your diary will become a mirror for other young people who, like you, are trying to understand how life should be lived. And *their* diaries and journals, though not yet written, will in turn become a mirror for still others not yet born! That common thread, tying together the lives of young diarists and journalists, holds fast the human spirit across the ages.

Published Diaries
Mentioned in This Book

BARBELLION, W. N. P. *The Journal of a Disappointed Man.* New York: George H. Doran Co., 1919.

BILLINGTON, RAY, ed. *The Journal of Charlotte Forten.* New York: Dryden Press, 1953.

BISHOP, ELIZABETH, ed. *The Diary of "Helena Morley."* New York: The Ecco Press, 1977.

CHENEY, EDNAH D., ed. *Louisa May Alcott: Her Life, Letters and Journals.* Boston: Little, Brown & Company, 1928.

FRANK, ANNE. *Anne Frank: The Diary of a Young Girl.* New York: Doubleday & Co., 1967.

GÁG, WANDA. *Growing Pains.* New York: Coward McCann, 1940.

HAVENS, CATHERINE ELIZABETH. *The Diary of a Little Girl in Old New York.* New York: Henry Collins Brown, 1920.

The Journal of Sarah Davenport. New Canaan, Connecticut: New Canaan Historical Society, 1950.

LAGERLÖF, SELMA. *The Diary of Selma Lagerlöf.* New York: Doubleday, Doran & Co., 1936.

LINDER, LESLIE, transcriber. *The Journal of Beatrix Potter.* London: Frederick Warne & Co., 1966.

MACBEAN, L. *Marjorie Fleming: The Story of Pet Marjorie Together with Her Journals and Her Letters.* New York: G. P. Putnam's Sons, 1904.

MAGOFFIN, SUSAN. *Down the Santa Fe Trail into Mexico: The Diary of Susan Shelby Magoffin, 1846–47.* New Haven: Yale University Press, 1926.

MUSSER, BENJAMIN. *The Diary of a Twelve Year Old.* Caldwell, Idaho: The Caxton Printers, 1932.

NEWBERRY, JULIA. *Julia Newberry's Diary.* New York: W. W. Norton, 1933.

NIN, ANAÏS. *Linotte: The Early Diary of Anaïs Nin.* New York: Harcourt, Brace, Jovanovich, 1980.

ROOSEVELT, THEODORE. *The Roosevelt Diaries of Boyhood and Youth.* New York: Charles Scribner's Sons, 1928.

SHORE, MARGARET EMILY. *The Journal of Emily Shore.* London: Kegan, Paul, Trench, Tribner & Co., 1891.

SHUTE, HENRY A. *The Real Diary of a Real Boy.* New York: The Baker & Taylor Co., 1917.

SLOANE, ERIC. *The Diary of an Early American Boy.* New York: Funk & Wagnalls, 1962.

STROUT, RICHARD LEE, ed. *Maud.* New York: The Macmillan Co., 1939.

THOMPSON, JAMES H., ed. *The Real Diary of a Rochester Boy.* Rochester, New York: n.p., 1917.

THOREAU, HENRY DAVID. *Walden.* New York: First Vintage Books/The Library of America Edition, 1991.

WINTHER, OSCAR OSBURN, ed. *With Sherman to the Sea: The Civil War Letters, Diaries and Reminiscences of Theodore F. Upson.* Baton Rouge, Louisiana: Louisiana State University Press, 1943.

WHITNEY, JANET. *Elizabeth Fry, Quaker Heroine.* Boston: Little, Brown & Co., 1937.

Index

97